"Love" Clear Album

by Janice Musante

Small transparent albums are wonderful to make and even more fun to share. Turn your imagination loose when adding your favorite embellishments to the pages.

SIZE: 4½" x 6"

MATERIALS:

Grafix Dura-Lar .005 clear film
• Photos • Decorative papers
• Paper flowers • Pebble brads
• Adhesive rhinestones • Stickers
• Rub-ons • Small silk flowers • Mini brads • Transparent overlays • 2 mm pearls • Three ½" diameter binder rings • Ribbons • *Tsukineko* Black Staz-On ink • Sharpie Black thin line marker • Needle and thread
• Die cuts • ⅛" hole punch
• Adhesive

Love - Front Cover
Mat photo, ink the edges and adhere to cover. Attach flowers with brads. Apply rub-ons and rhinestones.

Photo with Flower - page 1
Mat photo to cover the back of photo on the cover. Ink edges. Adhere the mounted photo directly over the back side of the photo on the front of the page, as shown. Adhere a flower with a button center over the brads of the flower from the cover.

Precious - page 2 Trim a transparency to fit the page. Attach to page at the corners with mini brads and small flowers. Mat photo and ink the edges. Adhere photo to page. Apply rub-ons.

INSTRUCTIONS:

Prep: Cut out six 4½" x 6" pages from Dura-Lar transparency film. Punch holes for the binding. Ink the page edges

Album Assembly: Punch 3 holes evenly along the left edge of each album page, ensuring that all the holes align. Attach pages with jump rings. Tie ribbons through closed rings. Adhere small flowers to ribbons. Use permanent black marker to dot the center of the flowers.

Photo - page 3

Ink the edges of the photo, mat, and adhere covering the back of the photo on the previous page; ink edges.

Cherish - page 4

Mat photo and ink edges. Adhere the photo to the page. Cut a paper strip, ink the edges and adhere to the left edge of the page. • Adhere a string of pearls to the lower edge. Attach printed paper flower and silk flower with a brad. Apply rub-ons and sticker. Cut a paper triangle, ink the edges and adhere to the corner.

Friend - page 5

Mat photo to fit over the back of the photo on the other side of the page. Ink the edges and adhere to page. Apply rub-ons and stickers to page.

Linked by Love - page 6

Mat photo, ink edges, and adhere to page. Apply resin corner stickers and rub-ons. Attach flower with a brad.

Photo with Flower - page 7
Ink photo edges, mat and adhere to page. Apply stick-on daisy to the page, centered over the back of the flower. Apply stickers to corners and page and adhere rhinestones to corners of photo.

Smile - page 8
Adhere photo to page. Apply rub-ons. Attach flower to page with a brad. Adhere Clear rhinestones. Apply corner sticker.

Because I Care - Back Cover
Ink paper edges and adhere over the photo back. Use a Black marker to write words. Apply rub-ons and stickers.

Photo with Flower - page 9
Ink edges of photo and mat to fit over the photo back from the other side. Adhere photo. Apply corner stickers and adhesive rhinestones to the backs of the rhinestones on the other side.

Togetherness - page 10
Adhere inked paper strips to the left edge of the page. Adhere photo. Apply rub-ons. Attach folded ribbons with a brad.

Rub-Ons - Rub-Ons really work great on clear pages. You can see the design right through both sides of the page. Rub design or word onto a clear acrylic page.

TIP: *Grafix* makes a terrific Rub-Onz Transfer Film. Simply run it through your computer to print inkjet images and words on the film. Rub the designs right onto almost anything.

TIP: *Design Originals* has a series of CDs available with digital images for scrolls, arrows, hearts, words, fonts, designs, etc... everything you need to make your own printouts of rub-ons... more economical then purchasing images separately.

At the Pier - Front Cover:
Mat photo with double-sided paper and ink edges. Adhere photo and papers to page from the back side. • Apply rub-ons and stickers to the front of the page. Attach chipboard die cuts and paper flowers with brads.

A Trip to Remember - page 1
Adhere stickers, rub-ons, and chipboard shapes to page.

Simple Pleasures - page 2
Mat photo with double-sided paper and ink edges. Adhere papers and photo to front of page. Adhere stickers and rub-ons to page.

Sunny Southern California
by Janice Musante
Summer colors, fun embellishments and simple titles allow you to revisit the pleasures of your vacation.
SIZE: 6" x 6"

MATERIALS:
Grafix Dura-Lar .007 clear film • Photos • Rub-Ons • Decorative papers • Epoxy stickers • Mini silk flowers • Die cuts • Stickers • Chipboard shapes • Brads • Embellishments • Rickrack • Ribbons • *Tsukineko* Black Staz-On ink • Thin line Black marking pen • Three 1" binder rings • ¼" hole punch • Adhesive

INSTRUCTIONS:
Prep: Cut out eight 6" x 6" pages from Dura-Lar transparency film; ink edges. Punch holes for the binding.

Assembly: Punch 3 holes along the left edge of each page. Thread a binder ring through each set of the holes and fasten. Tie ribbons to binder rings.

July - page 3
Mat photo, ink edges and adhere to page. Apply rub-ons and stickers.

Cute - page 4
Mat photo, ink edges and adhere to page. Apply rub-ons and sticker.

Grin - page 5
Mat photo, ink edges and adhere over the back of the photo that shows through the page. Apply stickers and rub-ons.

Ice Cream - page 6
Mat photos, ink edges and adhere to page. Apply stickers.

Carefree Summer Days - page 7
Mat photo and adhere to page. Mat stickers on cardstock and adhere to page. Adhere stickers and die cuts.

Vacation Fun - page 8
Mat photo. Adhere photo and papers together. Apply stickers. Do not adhere to page until you cover the back with materials for the next page.

What Fun - page 9
Mat photo. Adhere photo and papers to the back of papers for the previous page. Align Dura-Lar page over layout and attach paper flower with a brad. Adhere layout under the Dura-Lar. • Apply rub-ons and stickers to page.

Summer Lovin' - page 10
Mat photo and adhere to page. Attach flower to page with a brad. Adhere cut outs and draw ink lines around the edges. Apply rub-ons and stickers.

Beach - page 11
Adhere papers to page covering the back side of the photo. Adhere stickers and die cuts. Apply stickers. Attach flower with a brad.

Nature - page 12
Adhere papers to page. Mat photo, ink edges and adhere to page.
Apply stickers, die cuts and rub-ons. Adhere rickrack.

Fun Rides- page 13
Mat photo and adhere over the back of photo. Adhere die cuts. Apply stickers and rub-ons.

Vacation Moments- page 14
Ink photo edges and adhere to the page. Adhere die cuts. Apply stickers and rub-ons.

Sun & Sand - Back Cover
Adhere matted photo over the backside of the photo. Apply rub-ons and stickers.

Stamp on Clear - Rubber Stamps add wonderful details and images to clear pages. An added bonus is that the image shows on both sides of each page. Stamp designs with Staz-On Ink (a solvent base ink). Apply the rubber stamp image directly on the transparent film. allow to dry.

Tint on Clear - For a great look, tint the edges with a Staz-On Ink pad. Pat gently around the edges of the clear film with the ink pad or with a make-up sponge dipped in an ink pad. Allow to dry.

Our Wedding

by Vicki Chrisman

Create an elegant and unique transparent album that celebrates your special day.

SIZE: 6½" x 7½"

MATERIALS:
Pageframe Designs (clear tabs album, clear heart embellishment)
• Decorative papers • Vellum • Heart pins • Rub-ons • Tulle
• Lace • Adhesive rhinestones • Pearls on a string • Transparent overlays • *JudiKins* Diamond Glaze • Adhesive

Love - Front Cover
TIP: The key to planning the cover is to consider what will be seen on the pages behind. Adhere the photo and transparent overlay behind the cover to protect it from wear and tear. Also, plan for the colors on the inside pages to show through. Adhere lace and rhinestones to the outside of the cover.

Bouquet - page 1
Incorporate elements that show through from the previous side. Adhere photo to hide the back of the cover photo. Adhere lace and heart.

Cherish - page 2
Adhere papers, photo and rub-ons to page.

Kiley & Brad - page 3
A piece of transparent overlay, cut and tucked under the photo, adds design and interest to the backside of the paper showing through from the front of this page. Adhere photo. Print names and mat on paper. Adhere to page with lace. Add rhinestones.

Church Window - page 4
Adhere a strip of transparency under each side of the photo. Adhere rub-on to page tab.

Walking Down the Aisle - page 5
Adhere photo allowing the transparency from the other side to show.

I Take Thee Kiley For My Lawfully Wedded Wife - page 6
Crop the photos to fit the specific transparency shape you are using.

August 2007 - page 7
Adhere photo to cover the back of the preceding photo. Adhere rhinestones.

Presenting Mr. and Mrs. Helgenberger - page 8
Use bits and pieces of leftover rub-ons to add to your page. Adhere photo. Apply clear heart over photo.

Bride and Groom - page 9
Alternating the side of the page upon which you place the photo adds interest to the album.

Celebrate - page 10
Adhere photo and rub-ons.

Wedding Cakes - page 11
Planning the placement of photos allows an interesting layering effect. The cake page will appear to have two photos, but the bride and groom photo from page 9 will show through behind the cakes.

Father Daughter Dance - page 12
The sheer look of vellum works well with clear albums. Cut the ribbon long enough to cover the back of the page and tie off. Adhere vellum, photo, lace, rub-ons and rhinestones.

First Dance as a Couple - page 13
Adhere photo. Wrap lace from previous side of page and tie in a knot. Secure with tape. Tie sheer ribbon around the knot. Add rub-ons and rhinestone.

Just Married - page 14
Create a layout with photos, papers, rub-ons and ribbon. Add a clear heart shape, then turn the papers over and decorate the back for the cover before adhering to the page.

Add Clear Embellishments - Add clear acrylic tags and accents to your pages. These add fabulous dimension to your album and you can mark or rub on designs to embellish this clear item also.

Print Photos on Clear Film - Print your photos on *Grafix* Transparency Film (for inkjet printers). The photo will show twice, once on the front of the page and once again on the flip side.

Love is Kind - Back Cover
Adhere papers and rub-ons to the back side of the previous page layout. Then adhere to the acrylic so the acrylic protects the back cover of the book, preventing damage.

Album for Baby
by Kimber McGray
Baby photos are really fun to scrapbook. Make a small album for the grandparents too!

SIZE: 6½" x 7½"

MATERIALS:
Pageframe Designs clear tabs album • Chipboard • Flowers • Ribbons • Brads • Buttons • Clip • *Provo Craft* Chizzel-It Pen • *Crafters Workshop* scrolls template • Cream acrylic paint • Repositionable tape • Adhesive

Madison - Front Cover
Make etched scrolls on the cover. Add a chipboard heart and chipboard letter to the front cover with adhesive.

Inside the Cover - page 2
You'll be able to see this page through the front cover... really a fabulous way to show off your darling baby photos.
Attach a paper flower to the photo with a brad. Write the name with permanent Black ink. Adhere photo on the page.

I'm Fussy - page 3
Adhere photo covering the back of the photo on the previous side. Adhere chipboard heart over the heart from the other side.

Waking Up - page 4
Adhere photo to page. Adhere chipboard heart to photo. Write the birth date with a permanent pen.

INSTRUCTIONS:
Prep: For cover and all pages, - Using the Chizzel-It bullet tip, etch the design on a page. Remove template. Drybrush acrylic paint over 'the etched' design. Wipe off paint with a paper towel. The paint will stay in the etched portion of the design and make it show up better.
Assembly: Tie ribbons around the binder rings.

Pink Ribbon - page 5
Adhere photo covering the back of the photo on the previous side. Tie a ribbon to a clip and attach to photo. Adhere button to photo.

Three Buttons - page 6
Adhere photo to page. Adhere buttons to photo.

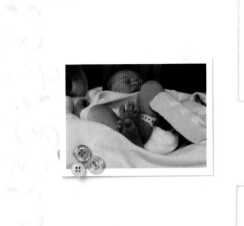

Mom and Baby - page 7
Adhere photo covering the back of the photo on the previous side. Adhere chipboard heart to photo.

Now We are Three - page 8
Adhere photo to page. Tie a ribbon to a clip and attach to photo.

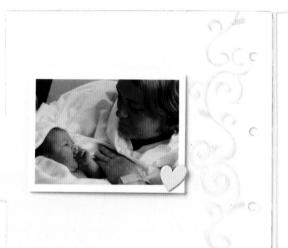

Etch on Clear Pages - Attach a scroll template to a Clear Album page with repositionable tape.

Etch on the Clear Page - Using the Chizzel-It bullet tip, etch the design on a page.

Remove Template - Remove the template.

Add Paint - Drybrush cream acrylic paint over the 'etched' design. Immediately wipe off the paint with a paper towel.

The paint will stay in the etched portion of the design and make it show up better.

Baby - Back Cover
Adhere a photo to the cover. Adhere a chipboard heart.

Frame - Front Cover:
Print the title on a transparency so that the photos are still fully visible.
TIP: Finish the cover of the album last.

Spring - page 2
Position the Transparency frame overlay.
Because the page is visible from both sides, cover the back of each photo with paper. This is a great journaling spot, so do your journaling before you adhere to the page. Adhere photo, papers, and rub-ons.

Four Seasons

by Betsy Veldman

I love children's books, especially the ones where parts of an entire scene are visible when the book is closed.

When this clever album is closed, you see all of the pictures, completing the "seasons" scene.

As you flip through the pages of the album, each photo has its own page and the journaling on the pages is hidden by the photos from the previous pages.

SIZE: 6½" x 7½"

MATERIALS:
Pageframe Designs clear tabs album • Digital Frames • Decorative papers • Rub-ons • Chipboard • Sticker Tabs • *Inque Boutique* rubber stamps • Transparency overlays • Embossing powder • *Tsukineko* StazOn ink pad • Computer Font: Sketchy • Adhesive

INSTRUCTIONS:
Prep: Create frames for the photos from digital elements and print them on transparency film.

Assembly: When putting the album together, position the pages on top of each other to get proper placement of the photos and embellishments, being careful that when the album is closed, all photos are visible.

Summer - pages 3 and 4

Position transparency frame. Adhere photo, papers, and rub-ons. Glossy Accents is a great adhesive to use on clear products. Just be sure to use small amounts.

Autumn - pages 5 and 6

TIP: When stamping or inking on clear projects, use StazOn ink. This is a permanent ink that will not smudge or smear when stamped on acrylic. Inking the acrylic edges makes them easier to see and handle. When stamping on acrylic, use light pressure so as not to smear the image and be sure to lift the stamp straight up off the project to avoid a "thick" or blurry image. • Position transparency frame. Adhere photo, papers, and rub-ons.

Winter - pages 7 and 8

Because this is the bottom page, it has the most coverage. Position transparency frame. Ink the edges of papers for added interest. Adhere photo, papers, and rub-ons.

Snapshots of You

by Michelle Van Etten

Lace, rhinestones, and intricate embellishments bring a touch of Victorian romance to this beautiful album.

SIZE: 6½" x 7½"

MATERIALS:

Pageframe Designs clear tabs album • Decorative papers • Stickers • Die cuts • Adhesive rhinestones • Flowers • Ribbons • Lace • Chipboard words • Rub-ons • *7gypsies* rubber stamp • *Hambly* Transparency overlay screen prints • *Mystic* bar code • Crown • *ColorBox* Cat's Eye Chalk ink • Adhesive

INSTRUCTIONS:

Prep: Create lots of drama and interest with your favorite embellishments.

Assembly: Be original... when putting the album together, pay attention as you position the embellishments to hide the back of elements on the previous page.

Snapshots of You - Front Cover

Adhere 2 photos back to back so one shows on the next page. Adhere lace along the spine. Repunch holes. Adhere photo, papers, die cut letters, flowers and rhinestones.

Tips for the Back Side ... How to Hide It

Because your pages are clear, special steps should be taken to hide adhesives or elements that show on the back side of pages.

Hide It - You can hide adhesives or elements by placing a photo and colored mat on the back.

You can also add cardstock, decorative paper or chipboard on the back. This is a great place to add journaling.

Or simply place a large flower or stickers. Often stickers come in pairs so you can place a mirror sticker on the back.

Beautiful Girl - page 1
Adhere papers, journaling box, lace, flowers and rhinestones to page.

Flower Collage - page 2
Use lace to hide the back side of the title. Adhere photo, papers, flowers and rhinestones to page.

Cherished Moments Journaling Page - page 3
Create a page so beautiful you won't be able to resist writing on it. Adhere papers, lace, flower, and rhinestones for extra sparkle.

Circular Frame - page 4
Adhere a printed transparency frame to the page and dress it up with added flowers, rhinestones, lace and chipboard letters. Adhere the lace and photo to the back of the transparency so it is sandwiched between the transparency and the page.

Baby of Mine - page 5
Adhere photo over the back of the photo on the other side. Adhere papers, lace, flower, and rhinestones.

Flower Child - page 6
Adhere photo to a large flower. Punch a hole and insert flower as a page.

Flower Child - page 7
Adhere photo to the back of the large flower to create another page.

Royalty - page 8
Adhere papers, photo, and rhinestones to page.

Savor the Moments - page 9
Adhere lace and photo to the back of the photo on the other side of the page. Add trim.

Happy Holidays - page 10
Adhere stamped tag and lace to flower. Punch a hole in a flower petal and insert into book as a page.

Holiday Flower - page 11
TIP: Using super large flowers for pages adds color, texture and depth to your album.

Santa - page 12
Layer and adhere papers and photos to page. Cover a photo with printed transparency or add rub-ons to highlight the photo. Adhere rhinestones, die cut flowers and ribbon.

Sweet - page 13
Layer and adhere papers and a photo to the page. Adhere rhinestones, flowers, ribbon and title.

Spring Flower - page 14
Adhere lace and a title to flower. Punch a hole in a petal and insert as a page.

Pink Flower - page 15
Adhere a photo to a flower center.

Play It Louder - page 16
The background papers on this page are actually adhered to the underside of the page. The photos, title, stickers, rub-ons and rhinestones are adhered to the surface of the page.

July - page 17
Cover the papers from the previous page. Add a flower, photo, lace and rhinestones. Stamp the title.

Flower - page 18
TIP: Purchase silk flowers in bunches and take them apart. Use different pieces throughout your album for a coordinated look.

Inside of Cover- page 1
The back of the pretty frame shows here.

Studying the Petals - page 2
Attach a transparency to page with eyelets. Adhere photo and flowers, then add rhinestone centers. Apply rub-on. Add the string of rhinestones along the bottom of the page after you adhere the wave on the next page so that you can follow the same path to hide the backside of the paper.

Flowers
by Kim Moreno

This is a must-have album for everyone who loves flowers.

SIZE: 6½" x 7½"

MATERIALS:
Pageframe Designs clear tabs album • Decorative papers • Transparency • Rub-ons • Chipboard • Flowers • Ribbon • Eyelets • Adhesive rhinestones • *Sharpie* White opaque pen • *Sakura* Micron pen • Crop-A-Dile • *Therm O Web* (Zots, ClicknStick)

INSTRUCTIONS:
Assembly: Open binder rings and insert a flower on each ring. Tie ribbons to each ring.

Flowers - Front Cover
Trim circle pattern from transparency and adhere to the cover. Cut a paper circle to fit inside of the center of the transparency. Adhere chipboard letters and rub-ons. Attach a flower with an eyelet. Use a White pen to freehand around the edge of the cover.

TIP: Hide the adhesive behind the patterns on the transparency.

Journal Page - page 3
Trim journaling paper to cover the back of the photo on the previous page. Add rhinestones and wavy strip of paper. Turn the page over and adhere the rhinestone strip over the wavy strip.

Makenna - page 4
Attach transparency to page with eyelets. Adhere papers, photo, rhinestones, and chipboard letters.

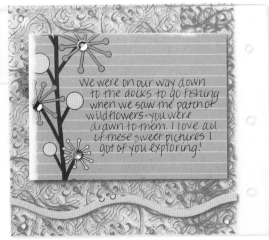 

For You - page 5
Adhere photo to page. Apply rub-on to help obscure the vertical photo from the previous page. Place a brad in the center of each cut out flower and adhere to page. Add rhinestones.

Sweet Girl - page 6
Trim circle pattern from the transparency, place photo behind it and adhere to page hiding the adhesive behind the patterns on the transparency. Adhere paper strip, photo, flowers, rhinestone centers, rub-ons and chipboard letters.

Wildflowers - page 7
Adhere photo to cover the photo from the previous page. Attach paper tabs to photo with brads. Adhere photo to page. Apply rub-ons.

Inside of Back Cover
Attach transparency with eyelets. Adhere circle and rub-ons to page. Record the date and place with a White opaque pen.

 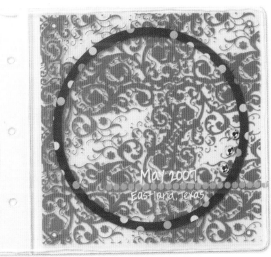

Add Sheer Ribbon - Sheer ribbon or lace trim looks great when you attach it to a clear page. Stitch, glue or attach sheer Organza type ribbon to the surface of a page for a fabulous look.

Transparency Overlays - Secure transparencies with brads or eyelets for unique images. *Hambly* screen print Transparencies are perfect for this. Cut out images and words to use on several pages.
TIP: *Grafix* makes Transparency film so you can print out your images, words and photos on a computer.

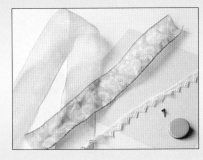 

Explore

by Vicki Chrisman

Explore the possibilities and promise of the world around you and record the experience in an unforgettable album.

SIZE: 6½" x 7½"

MATERIALS:

Pageframe Designs Clear tabs album • Papers • Chipboard • Rub-ons • Buttons • *Sharpie* White opaque pen • *Jacquard* Lumiere paints • Adhesive rhinestones • *JudiKins* Diamond Glaze • Adhesive

INSTRUCTIONS:

Assembly: Open binder rings to attach the pages together in an album.

Explore - Front Cover

Adhere chipboard and button. Use a White pen to make dots for the stem. The photo is seen through from the next page.

Tips for Drawing and Journaling with Markers

Trace Patterns - For accurate writing, tape a pattern, design or word under a clear page. Trace right over the pattern.

Doodling - Draw freehand scrolls, lines and marks. Or you can mark through plastic design templates or trace over a pattern.

Souffle Pens - At first you won't see the Souffle ink. Be patient and after a minute the ink will appear. It is like magic.

Slick Writers - These pens have fine tips and make wonderful marks. They are great for journaling, and come in several colors.

Kirstyn 2007 - page 1
Adhere chipboard flower centers to hide the adhesive from the other side of the page. Cover the backs of the title with the name and date labels.

Be Happy - page 2
Incorporate doodling with a Sharpie and flower rub-ons on the patterned paper attached to the underside of the page. Adhere the photo leaving a space for a strip of decorative rub-on.

Be True - page 3
Take advantage of the design on the front by mirroring it on the back. Create labels for the front and back of the tab. Adhere them, back to back and then adhere to the tab so the front label shows through from the underside.

Curiosity - page 4
Cover the page with double-sided paper so it shows through for use on the next page. Adhere photo. Add cut out shapes and fibers.

Beauty - page 5
Apply rub-on border. Adhere paper strip and photo. Stamp a title and adhere it to the page.

Simple Things - page 6
Print words on cardstock and cut out. Adhere photo and words to page. Adhere a label to the tab.

Take Flight - page 7
Adhere photo, chipboard wings, and printed words. Notice how the wings show through on both sides and are placed to complement both photographs.

Dream - page 8
Paint chipboard with Lumiere. Let dry. Adhere chipboard, rub-on, rhinestones, and printed word.

Butterfly - page 9
Adhere rhinestones over the ones on the previous side to hide the adhesive.

Transparency - page 10
Punch holes in a printed transparency overlay and insert into the album for an interesting overlay.

Rays of Love - page 11
You'll see the images of the printed transparency overlay from page 10.

Travel - page 12
Adhere photo, flower sticker and rhinestone. The paper circle shows through from the next page. Apply the rub-on in the center after adding the circle on the back.

Live - page 13
Adhere photo and paper border. Cut a circle from double-sided paper and adhere to page. Stamp design and add printed word. Turn the page over and apply the rub-on over the circle. Apply label to the tabs.

Play All Day - page 14
Print words to fit page. Adhere photo and words, leaving an open space for the next photo to show through.

Rosy Cheeks - page 15
Mirror image the photo and paper border from the previous side.

Sunkissed - page 16
Adhere photo and apply rub-ons. Cover tab with paper.

Play - page 17
Print words on card-stock and cut out. Adhere words and photo to page.

Live, Dream, Explore - page 18
Adhere double-sided paper so it shows through to the back cover. Adhere photo and printed words to page. Adhere ribbon all the way around both sides of the cover, tying in a knot on the outside of the book.

Cherish

*by Michele Charles
and Paula Phillips*

Are you in the mood for something simple, something fun, and something different? Try an album with pages in graduated widths. Alcohol inks and masking make this an intriguing project with awesome results.

SIZE: 5" x 7½"

MATERIALS:

Midnight Oil Scrapbook Designs clear album • Cardstock • 3 binder rings • Ribbon • Snaps • Brads • Stickers • Adhesive flowers • *Heidi Swapp* Cherish stamp • *Tsukineko* Black StazOn ink • Silver pen • Black marker • *Ranger* (Alcohol ink applicator, Felt, Cut n' Dry foam, ¼" wide Silver Adhesive Foil tape, Adirondack Alcohol inks - Stream, Butterscotch, Wild Plum) • Aluminum tape • *JudiKins* Eclipse tape • Punches (1" circle, Butterfly) • Adhesive

INSTRUCTIONS:

Assembly: Add a snap to the upper corner of each page. Align 3 holes in the left side of each page. Thread binder rings through the holes. Tie ribbons around the binder rings.

INSTRUCTIONS:

Prep for Black page 1: Punch circles from Eclipse tape. Place circles onto the back side of the page. Using foam, cover the entire surface of the back page with StazOn Black ink. Let dry. Remove the circle masks.

Prep for Marbled pages 2 & 4: On the back side, cover with several colors of alcohol ink. Drip a dime size amount of ink onto felt and dab onto the clear acrylic page. Let dry. Cover edges with aluminum tape.

Prep for Black page 3: Punch butterflies from Eclipse tape. Place butterflies onto the back side of the page. Using foam, cover the entire surface of the back page with StazOn Black ink. Let dry. Remove the butterfly masks. Cover edges with aluminum tape.

TIP: Here's a fantastic look for your photos. When you leave the clear circles on any clear page, add circle photos behind some of the circles. This gives a hide and seek mystery to the album page.

Color Clear Pages with Ink

Prep for Black pages 1 and 3: Punch circles and butterflies from Eclipse tape. Place circles and butterflies onto the back side of the clear pages.

Using foam, cover the entire surface of the clear page with StazOn black ink. Let dry. Remove the circle and butterfly masks.

Prep for Marbled pages 2 & 4: Cover the back side of the clear pages with several colors of Alcohol ink.

Drip a dime size amount of ink onto felt and dab onto the clear acrylic page. Repeat with another color, and then another color. Let dry.

Cover the edges with aluminum tape.

**Smile
- Front Cover**
Ink the back of a piece of *Grafix* Dura-Lar clear film as you did with the pages. Cover with aluminum tape and tape the edges. Adhere a photo in the center and adhere piece to the page.
Adhere small photos behind the circles.

**Cowgirl Kaylee
- page 1**
Mat a photo, add metal embellishments and adhere to page. Use a sticker and a Silver pen to create the name plate. Adhere the name plate so it shows through one of the circles on the cover.

**Butterflies
- page 2**
Mat a photo and adhere to page. Attach layered flowers together with brads and adhere to page.

**Cherish
- page 3**
Crop photo in a circle. Cut a circular mat and adhere to page.
Write the word with a marker and cut out. Adhere to page.

Each page is a different width... to make a waterfall effect and see all the photos at one time.

My 3 Boys - Front Cover
Create a title with rub-ons and a foam sticker.

Stars Book
by Kim Moreno
Unique shapes are always more interesting than the everyday square. This Stars book is a shining example.

SIZE: 8" x 8¼"

MATERIALS:
Pageframe Designs clear stars album • Decorative papers • Cardstock • Transparencies • Eyelets • Foam letter • Rub-ons • Chipboard stars • Brads • *Fontwerks* stamp • *ColorBox* ink • Adhesive

INSTRUCTIONS:

Prep for Small Stars:
Use the small clear star as a template to make 3 double-sided paper stars.
Cover the chipboard stars with paper on one side, and stamp circles on the front. Insert a brad in the center of the star. Adhere to the front of the clear star.
Turn the clear star over and apply glue on the back of the star only where the chipboard star shows through. Adhere the paper star to the back of the clear star. Journal on the back of the stars.

Prep for Large Stars: Using the large star as a template, cut 4 stars from printed transparency film.

Assembly: Punch a hole in the top of each star. Thread stars onto a binder ring alternating large and small stars. Begin and end with a large star.

Large Stars

Trim mat and photos to fit on each star. Adhere a photo on the front of each star. Adhere the mat on the underside of the star, hiding the adhesive between photo and mat. Layer the transparency star on the back, sandwiching the mat. Secure layers with eyelets.

Small Stars

Journal on the back of each small star.

Assembly: Punch a hole in the top of each star. Thread stars onto a binder ring alternating large and small stars. Begin and end with a large star.

**My 3 Boys
Are the Stars
in My Life...**

Large Stars: Using the large star as a template, cut 4 stars from printed transparency film.

TIP: Trim mat and photos to fit on each star. Adhere a photo on the front of each star. Adhere a mat on the underside of the star, hiding the adhesive between photo and mat.

Layer the transparency star on the back, sandwiching the mat. Secure layers with eyelets.

Vicki Chrisman

Paper Crafting has been Vicki's passion for over 15 years. Her work has been featured on the covers of "Altered Art" and "Paper ART" magazines. She was Creating Keepsakes, May 2007 "Fresh Face" and was part of the initial Design Team for Scrapbook Answers Magazine. She designs for Crafty Secrets Heartwarming Vintage, Fancy Pants Designs, AccuCut, and Pageframe Designs.

Punch Holes in Clear Pages - Use a hand punch (Whale of a Punches work great) to make decorative holes in clear pages. Stitch in the holes, attach binder rings, brads and eyelets.

Make Holes in Clear Pages - Use a Crop-a-Dile tool to make holes in clear pages. Make a series of holes for a great look or attach items in the holes.

Betsy Veldman

Betsy has been scrapbooking and papercrafting for seven years. Her work has appeared in many publications including Scrapbooks, Etc., Scrapbook Trends, Memory Makers, Paper Crafts. Her style is mostly graphic, but she loves to add unexpected touches to her projects. She works for several manufacturers including Picture It Page Frames.

To see more of her work visit www.scrapbookresumes.com/BetsyVeldman.

Janice Musante

Janice has thirty-two years in the field of education. A graduate of the Fashion Institute of Technology with a degree in art, Janice is enjoying her "artistic roots" with her current designs. Her designs have been published in card and craft magazines. Her creativity and innovation with clearly transparent cards and scrapbook albums is truly amazing. She loves the clear acrylic films, Rub Onz and Transparency sheets from Grafix.

MANY THANKS to my friends for their
cheerful help and wonderful ideas!
Kathy Mason • Donna Kinsey • Paula Phillips
Janet Long • Patty Williams • David & Donna Thomason

Meet the Designers

These top designers share special tips and hints throughout the book. Look for all the great helpful hints in the colored boxes.

Michelle Van Etten

Michelle enjoys teaching all over the world. Her passion for scrapbooking started as a way to showcase her family photos in a more unique way and tell the story behind the photos. Her work can be seen in Paper Arts, Memory Makers, Legacy, FW Books, company catalogs, and The Complete Idiot's Guide to Scrapbook Illustration and Altered Art.

Kimber McGray

2007 winner of Creating Keepsakes Hall of Fame, Kimber currently designs for We R Memory Keepers, Pageframe Designs, Serendipity Kits, and Homegrown Scrapbooks. She also teaches classes at her local scrapbook store. Her work has been published in Making Memories, Creating Keepsakes, BHG Scrapbooks etc., Scrapbook Trends, Cards, Scrapbook and Cards Today.
You can view her work at www.scrapbookframe.com/gallery.

Kimberly Moreno

Kim has been scrapbooking for over 7 years, with features in many publications including Creating Keepsakes, Scrapbook Trends, Memory Makers, Paper Crafts and more. She is co-owner and design team coordinator for Pageframe Designs and a member of several manufacturer teams.
To see more of her work visit www.scrapbookresumes.com/Kim Moreno/

Michele Charles

One of the most effervescent, exciting, and effective teachers of multi-media in the industry today,
Michele travels across the country bringing her energetic presentation style and sense of humor to workshops that are loaded with innovative techniques.
For more information, visit Michele's website at www.michelecharles.com.

Clear Adhesives for Clear Pages

It is important to adhere items to clear pages with special clear adhesives. We tested many glues and adhesives for adhesion and clarity. Listed below are our favorites.

Diamond Glaze   *by JudiKins*
Fusion   *by Duncan*
Glossy Accents   *by Ranger*
Double Stick Tape *by Scotch*
Zots   *by ThermoWeb.*
E6000 or Goop   *by Eclectic*
Scrapbook Adhesive *by 3L.*
Pink Terrific Tape *by Provo Craft*

Special Markers for Clear Album Pages

Use pens and markers to journal, doodle, outline, penstitch and add titles. You can also add interesting color on clear pages.

It is important to mark on clear pages with special markers. We tested many markers and pens for adhesion and opacity. Listed below are our favorites.

Slicker Writers for Journaling
by American Crafts

Souffle Pens for Doodling
by American Crafts

Opaque Stix
by Marvy-Uchida

Permopaque Pens for Doodling
by Sakura

Sharpie Pens - Ultra fine point
by Sanford

Sharpie Pens - Fine point
by Sanford

Sharpie Pens - Metallics, fine tip
by Sanford

Sharpie Pens - Paint Pens
by Sanford

DecoColor - Fine tip
by Marvy-Uchida

Apply a Mask - Apply a mask such as masking tape, paper or a Heidi Swapp self-adhesive scroll or flower mask.

Spray Paint - Hold a can of spray paint about 12" from the surface and spray color onto the clear acrylic page. Be sure to protect your work surface with newspapers and work in a ventilated area. Allow paint to dry.

Remove the Mask - Pull off the mask to reveal clear areas on each page.

Summer Fun

by Kimber McGray

There are so many joys of summer! Capture them all in a memory book that will make you smile all winter long.

You'll love Kimber's clever spray paint technique. With paint you can add color to clear pages quickly, and you'll have wonderful "windows" of clear areas on each page and on the cover.

SIZE: 6½" x 7½"

MATERIALS:
Pageframe Designs Acrylic tabs album • Stickers • Chipboard letters • Rub-ons • Ribbon • Rickrack • Pen • *Krylon* spray paint (Blue and Red) • *Heidi Swapp* scrolls and flower self-adhesive mask • Adhesive

INSTRUCTIONS:
Prep: Lay self-adhesive mask on one side of each page. Spray with paint. Let dry. Remove mask.

Assembly: Tie ribbons and rickrack to binder rings.

Summer Fun - Front Cover
The page will already be red with masked scrolls and flowers. Apply rub-ons, stickers, and adhere chipboard letters.

**Inside of Cover
- page 1**

The masked scrolls and flowers will show through.

**Summer 07
- page 2**

Adhere photo to page. Write notes in the painted circles and the date on the tab with a pen.

**I'm Thirsty
- page 3**

Adhere photo over the back of the photo on the other side of the page.

**Badminton Pro
- page 4**

Adhere photo to page. Journal with a pen.

**Berries & Cream
- page 5**

Adhere photo over the back of the photo on the other side of the page. Add journal notes with a pen.

**Ice Cream Cones
- page 6**

Adhere photos to page. Journal with a pen.

Gardening - page 7
Adhere photos over the back of the photos on the other side of the page. Add journal notes with a pen.

Playground Favorites - page 8
Adhere photo to page. Journal with a pen.

Chalk Drawing - page 9
Adhere photos over the back of the photos on the other side of the page. Add journal notes with a pen.

Sprinkler Park - page 10
Adhere photos to page. Journal with a pen.

Suppliers - Most scrapbook stores carry an excellent assortment of supplies. If you need something special, ask your local store to contact the following companies.

Dura-Lar, Transparency & rub-on film - Grafix,
Clear Albums, Acrylic Stars - Pageframe Designs, Midnight Oil Scrapbook Designs
Adhesive - JudiKins, Ranger, 3L, Beacon, Therm O Web, Duncan, Eclectic Products
Rubber stamps - 7gypsies, Fontwerks, Heidi Swapp, Inque Boutique

Tips for Adhesives ... How to Attach Accents

Diamond Glaze - This adhesive is very clear and makes a fine thin line of glue. It works best with flat and paper accents.

Glossy Accents - This adhesive makes a clear line with a bit of bulk. It works best with flat paper accents & with small ribbon.

Fusion - This adhesive squeezes out in a nice line with a bit of bulk. It works well with paper accents and silk flowers.

E6000 & Goop - These tube glues squeeze out in small globs or pads of glue. The pads work with dimensional accents.